This guide belongs to:

_____

Date:

_____

Contents

Contents

By understanding our Creator
and seeking after Him,
we will find
our true identity and
learn how to love God and
ourselves
wholeheartedly.

Hi there,

Today is a fantastic day to start the
journey of loving your life. We search for
love all around us and extend love to
other people, but the last person
we tend to take the time to get to know
and love is ourselves. So, through this
30-day guide, we will examine
our lives and focus on loving
ourselves as God intended through daily
reflection, physical activities, and
spending time with God. We cannot
go on this journey without the Creator
of love and love Himself, God.
We will build our lives on Him as our
foundation and go to the Word of God
to understand how God intended
for us to love. By the end of this journey,
you'll have experienced God's
unshakeable love and obtain a love for
your life that will last forever since it
will be built on our eternal God. Feel free
to reread this guide as much as possible.

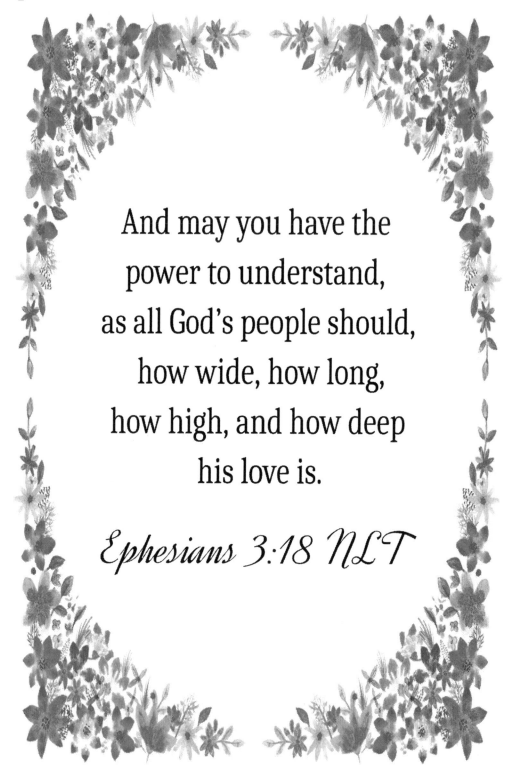

And may you have the
power to understand,
as all God's people should,
how wide, how long,
how high, and how deep
his love is.

Ephesians 3:18 NLT

Day 1:

The love of God

The love of God

Focus of the day

The love of God is simple, comforting, extensive, everlasting, and perfect. God is enamored with us. He is our Father, and we are His children. God's love for us is so unwavering that it motivates us to learn more about God and ourselves. How can a holy and eternal God love us sinners endlessly? Because God is love. He cannot be anything besides Himself. Therefore, God is the only one we should pursue and evaluate concerning love. God is tremendously excited to speak with you, ready to assist you in discovering who you genuinely are and enlighten you on how to love.

Tasks for the day

Spend time with God for 30 minutes. Thank God for His love. Bask in the love of God and invite Him into your space. Focus on embracing His love and learning more about our wonderful Savior. Read 1 Corinthians 13; Ephesians 3:17-19; 1 John 4:19.

Let's get moving

Whole body stretch for 30 minutes. Spend 30 minutes outside. Drink 1 gallon of water.

Date: ....

Reflection

Today, I am truly grateful for...

_____

_____

_____

What I love about myself...

_____

_____

_____

_____

_____

What I learned about myself today...

_____

_____

_____

_____

_____

I am...

_____

_____

_____

I forgave myself today for...

_____

_____

What I would like to change about myself...

_____

_____

An amazing thing that happened today...

_____

DATE

My time with God

| TODAY'S PASSAGE | BIBLE VERSION | TODAY'S TOPIC |

NOTES

KEY VERSES

PRAYER

KEY POINTS

APPLICATION

Let's get things done!

TOP PRIORITIES	IDEAS	WATER

DC250ML

TO-DO	THOUGHTS	FOOD

		BREAKFAST	LUNCH	DINNER

	RELAXING THINGS TO DO	GOALS

FITNESS	NOTES	

SKETCH

Notes

Notes

Do not conform to the
pattern of this world,
but be transformed by
the renewing of
your mind. Then you
will be able to test
and approve what
God's will is—his good,
pleasing and
perfect will.

Romans 12:2 NIV

Day 2:

Renewing

the mind

Renewing the mind

Focus of the day

To begin loving yourself more, you must renew your mind. There are beliefs and boundaries we adhere to that are intended to keep us from loving ourselves. We must address the imaginations and memories we have as well. Futhermore, our thoughts are powerful and can significantly impact how we live. Our thoughts can be influenced by God, the enemy, people, or our past. Therefore, to renew our minds, we must take our thoughts captive and replace them with the word of God. Hold your thoughts up against the word of God and ask, "Did this come from God?" And if it did not, it must go.

Tasks for the day

Spend time with God for 30 minutes. Ask God to renew your mind today. Write down any thought that does not reflect God and declare 2 Corinthians 10:5 over it. Read Matthew 15:13; Romans 12; 1 Corinthians 6:10; 2 Corinthians 10; Philippians 4.

Let's get moving

Exercise for 30 minutes. Spend 30 minutes outside. Drink 1 gallon of water.

Date: _____   *Reflection*

Today, I am truly grateful for...

What I love about myself...

What I learned about myself today...

I am...

I forgave myself today for...

What I would like to change about myself...

An amazing thing that happened today...

My time with God

DATE _____

TODAY'S PASSAGE	BIBLE VERSION	TODAY'S TOPIC

NOTES
_____
_____
_____
_____
_____
_____
_____
_____
_____

KEY VERSES

PRAYER
_____
_____
_____
_____
_____
_____

KEY POINTS

_____
_____
_____
_____
_____
_____
_____

APPLICATION

Let's get things done!

TOP PRIORITIES	IDEAS	WATER

TO-DO	THOUGHTS	FOOD

BREAKFAST	LUNCH	DINNER

	RELAXING THINGS TO DO	GOALS

FITNESS	NOTES	

		SKETCH

Notes

Notes

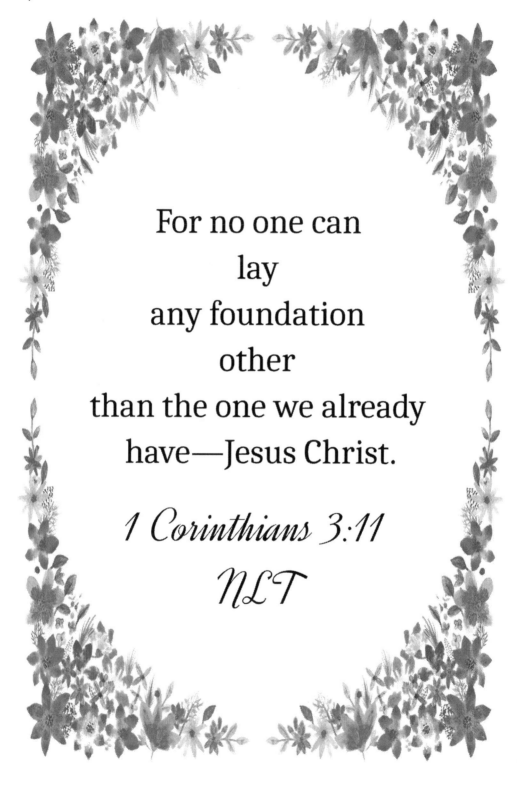

For no one can
lay
any foundation
other
than the one we already
have—Jesus Christ.

1 Corinthians 3:11

NLT

Day 3:

Christ is our foundation

Christ is our foundation

Focus of the day

Now that we have renewed our minds and removed every thought that challenged the Word of God, it is time to rest on the foundation already set for us, Jesus Christ. He is our firm foundation. Our thoughts, imaginations, and perspectives should only look like Him since we are planted in Jesus.

Tasks for the day

Spend time with God for 30 minutes.
Get to know God as your firm foundation by meditating on the heart of God. Walk with Jesus today and share your thoughts and feelings with Him. Read Proverbs 10:25; Matthew 7; 1 Corinthians 3.

Let's get moving

Exercise for 30 minutes.
Spend 30 minutes outside.
Drink 1 gallon of water.

Date: ....

Reflection

Today, I am truly grateful for...
_____
_____
_____

What I love about myself...
_____
_____
_____
_____
_____

What I learned about myself today...
_____
_____
_____
_____

I am...
_____
_____

I forgave myself today for...
_____
_____

What I would like to change about myself...
_____
_____

An amazing thing that happened today...
_____

My time with God

DATE

TODAY'S PASSAGE

BIBLE VERSION

TODAY'S TOPIC

NOTES

KEY VERSES

KEY POINTS

PRAYER

APPLICATION

Let's get things done!

TOP PRIORITIES	IDEAS	WATER

DC250ML

TO-DO	THOUGHTS	FOOD

		BREAKFAST	LUNCH	DINNER

	RELAXING THINGS TO DO	GOALS

FITNESS	NOTES	

SKETCH

Notes

Notes

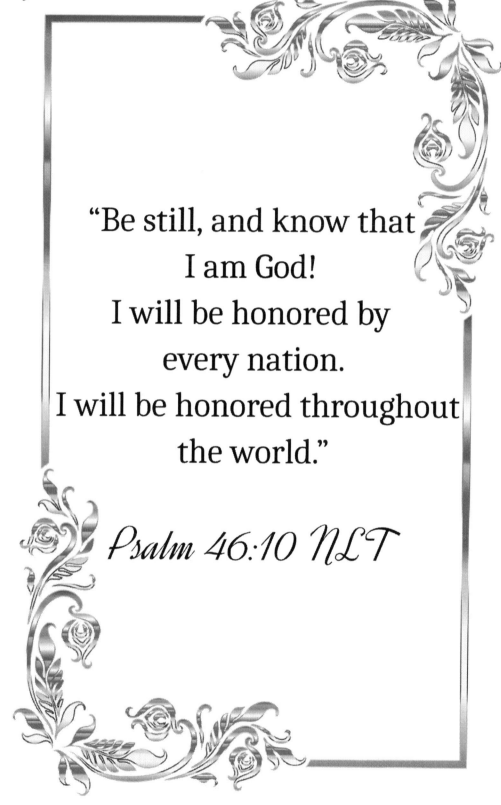

"Be still, and know that
I am God!
I will be honored by
every nation.
I will be honored throughout
the world."

Psalm 46:10 NLT

Day 4:

Do nothing

day

Do nothing day

Focus of the day

Doing nothing is doing something.
Having a day to do nothing is essential.
It's a time to relax our minds and
rest. Today is a day to take in your
surroundings and just be present. Leave every
worry, concern, task, and project where
it is, and breathe.

Tasks for the day

Spend time with God for 30 minutes.
Relax today. Go outside and enjoy nature.
Watch a movie. Eat your favorite meal.
Do something today that relaxes your mind
and honors God.
Read Colossians 1 and 3.

Let's get moving

Full body stretch for 30 minutes.
Spend 30 minutes outside.
Drink 1 gallon of water.

Date: .... *Reflection*

Today, I am truly grateful for...

_____
_____

What I love about myself...

_____
_____
_____
_____

What I learned about myself today...

_____
_____
_____

I am...

_____
_____

I forgave myself today for...

_____
_____

What I would like to change about myself...

_____
_____

An amazing thing that happened today...

_____

DATE _____

My time with God

TODAY'S PASSAGE   BIBLE VERSION   TODAY'S TOPIC

NOTES

_____

_____

_____

_____

_____

_____

_____

_____

_____

_____

_____

KEY VERSES

PRAYER

_____

_____

_____

_____

_____

_____

KEY POINTS

_____

_____

_____

_____

_____

_____

_____

APPLICATION

Let's get things done!

TOP PRIORITIES	IDEAS	WATER

TO-DO	THOUGHTS	FOOD

BREAKFAST | LUNCH | DINNER

	RELAXING THINGS TO DO	GOALS

FITNESS	NOTES	

SKETCH

Notes

Notes

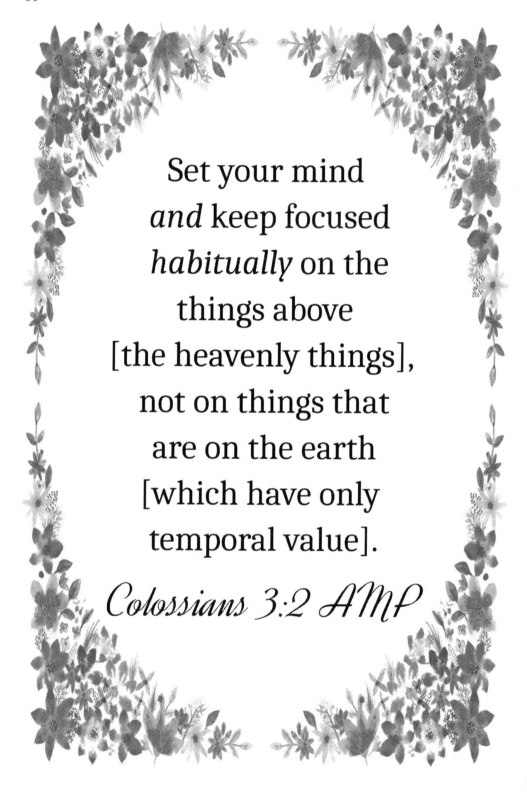

Set your mind
and keep focused
habitually on the
things above
[the heavenly things],
not on things that
are on the earth
[which have only
temporal value].

Colossians 3:2 AMP

Day 5:

Add

life-giving

thoughts

Add life-giving thoughts

Focus of the day

The Word of God is life. His Word can change any situation and transform our lives. So, today we are focusing on taking the Word of God and making it our thoughts. When we take the time to meditate and memorize the Word of God, it will always be in our minds and speech. Eventually, we will find our lives changing daily as we allow the Word of God to take over our minds completely.

Tasks for the day

Spend time with God for 30 minutes. Meditate and memorize the scriptures for today. Speak the Word of God today and allow His Word to make you over entirely. Picture God washing and purifying you with His Word. Read Proverbs 4:20-27; Philippians 4:8; Colossians 3:1-14.

Let's get moving

Exercise for 30 minutes. Spend 30 minutes outside. Drink 1 gallon of water.

Date: ....

Reflection

Today, I am truly grateful for...

What I love about myself...

What I learned about myself today...

I am...

I forgave myself today for...

What I would like to change about myself...

An amazing thing that happened today...

My time with God

DATE _____

| TODAY'S PASSAGE | BIBLE VERSION | TODAY'S TOPIC |

NOTES
_____
_____
_____
_____
_____
_____
_____
_____
_____
_____

PRAYER
_____
_____
_____
_____
_____
_____
_____

_____
_____
_____
_____
_____
_____
_____
_____

KEY VERSES

KEY POINTS

APPLICATION

Let's get things done!

TOP PRIORITIES	IDEAS	WATER

TO-DO	THOUGHTS	FOOD

BREAKFAST	LUNCH	DINNER

	RELAXING THINGS TO DO	GOALS

FITNESS	NOTES	

SKETCH

Notes

Notes

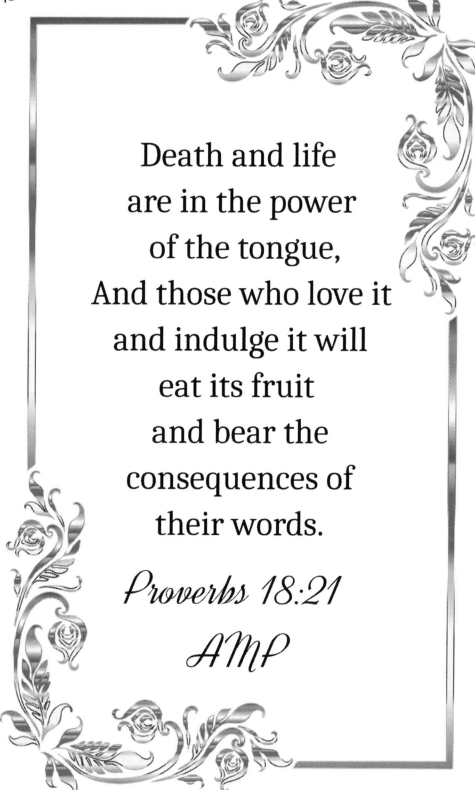

Death and life
are in the power
of the tongue,
And those who love it
and indulge it will
eat its fruit
and bear the
consequences of
their words.

Proverbs 18:21

AMP

Day 6:

Speak

life

Speak life

Focus of the day

Speak life! Prophesy! Speak the Word of God and declare His promises over your life. Since our thoughts are filled with life-giving thoughts, so shall our speech be filled with life. By speaking life/the Word of God, situations and circumstances must bow down to what you say since everything bows down to the Word of God. God already gave us these wonderful promises, so we must agree by declaring them out loud over our lives.

Tasks for the day

Spend time with God for 30 minutes. Prophesy and declare the Word of God today. Believe that what you have declared has already come to pass in your life. Declare Ezekiel 37:4-14 over everything in your life. Read Proverbs 18 and Ezekiel 37.

Let's get moving

Exercise for 30 minutes.
Spend 30 minutes outside.
Drink 1 gallon of water.

Date: _____

Reflection

Today, I am truly grateful for...

_____

_____

_____

What I love about myself...

_____

_____

_____

_____

_____

What I learned about myself today...

_____

_____

_____

_____

_____

I am...

_____

_____

_____

I forgave myself today for...

_____

_____

_____

What I would like to change about myself...

_____

_____

An amazing thing that happened today...

_____

DATE

My time with God

TODAY'S PASSAGE   BIBLE VERSION   TODAY'S TOPIC

NOTES

KEY VERSES

PRAYER

KEY POINTS

APPLICATION

Let's get things done!

TOP PRIORITIES	IDEAS	WATER

TO-DO	THOUGHTS	FOOD

	BREAKFAST	LUNCH	DINNER

	RELAXING THINGS TO DO	GOALS

FITNESS	NOTES	

		SKETCH

Notes

Notes

"Keep the
Sabbath day holy.
Don't pursue your own
interests on that day, but
enjoy the Sabbath and speak
of it with delight as the
Lord's holy day. Honor the
Sabbath in everything you
do on that day, and don't
follow your own
desires or talk idly.

Isaiah 58:13

NLT

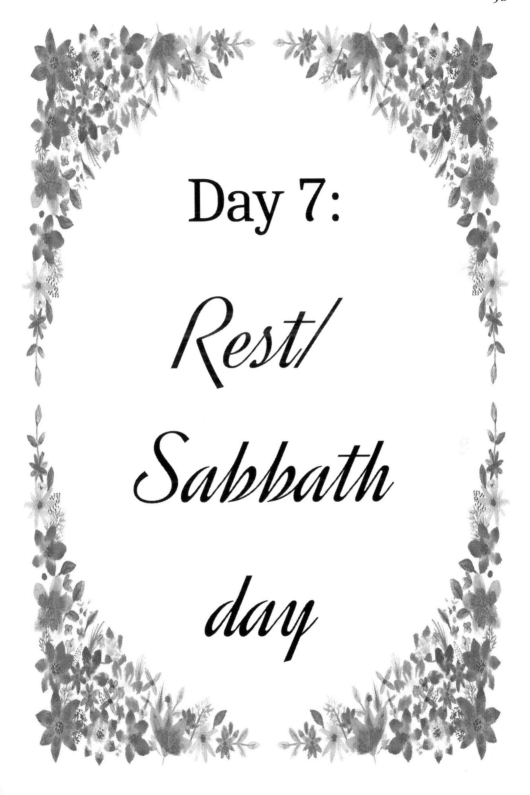

Day 7:

Rest/

Sabbath

day

Rest/Sabbath day

Focus of the day

Rest/ sabbath is a holy day, and we must
keep this day holy. On the seventh day,
God rested after completing the heavens and
earth. Therefore, we should follow our Father by
resting as He did, not performing any work on
this day, reflecting, and remembering all God
has done. It is a day to honor God and thank
Him for the life and gifts He has given us.
So, let's rest, refocus and remember God today.

Tasks for the day

Spend time with God for 30 minutes.
Reflect on the goodness of Jesus today and honor
him by devoting your time to remembering
all he has done for you. Imagine Jesus sitting next
to you as you reflect on your answered prayers.
Talk to Him like He's in the room with you
because He is. Read Genesis 1; 2:1-2; Psalm 92;
Isaiah 58:13-14.

Let's get moving

Dance to worship music for 30 minutes.
Walk for 30 minutes outside. Drink 1 gallon of
water and eat a salad with each meal.

Date: ....

Reflection

Today, I am truly grateful for...

_____

_____

_____

What I love about myself...

_____

_____

_____

_____

What I learned about myself today...

_____

_____

_____

_____

I am...

_____

_____

_____

I forgave myself today for...

_____

_____

What I would like to change about myself...

_____

_____

An amazing thing that happened today...

_____

My time with God

DATE

TODAY'S PASSAGE   BIBLE VERSION   TODAY'S TOPIC

NOTES

KEY VERSES

PRAYER

KEY POINTS

APPLICATION

Let's get things done!

TOP PRIORITIES	IDEAS	WATER

TO-DO	THOUGHTS	FOOD

BREAKFAST	LUNCH	DINNER

	RELAXING THINGS TO DO	GOALS

FITNESS	NOTES	

		SKETCH

Notes

Notes

I say, 'You are gods;
you are all children
of the Most High.

Psalms 82:6 NLT

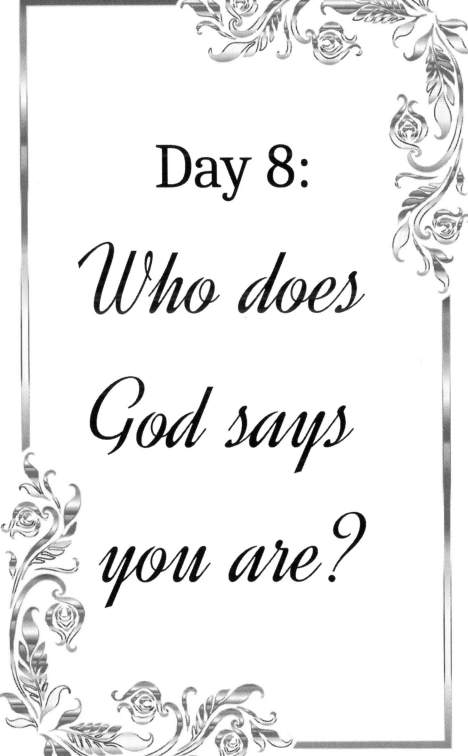

Day 8:

Who does

God says

you are?

Who does God say you are?

Focus of the day

When God looks at us, He sees His children and has eternal love for us. God calls us His treasure and masterpiece. His love for us is so deep and nothing can separate us from it. As we continue to pursue God, we will perceive and love ourselves the way He loves us. Through the eyes of the Creator, we can see the beauty and love in His creation.

Tasks for the day

Spend time with God for 30 minutes. Write out scriptures on what God says about you. Invite God to sit with you to review the scriptures for today. Declare those scriptures over your life until you believe them. Read Psalm 139; Romans 8; 1 Corinthians 13.

Let's get moving

Exercise for 30 minutes. Spend 30 minutes outside. Drink 1 gallon of water and drink a healthy smoothie as a snack.

Reflection

Date: ....

Today, I am truly grateful for...

What I love about myself...

What I learned about myself today...

I am...

I forgave myself today for...

What I would like to change about myself...

An amazing thing that happened today...

DATE

My time with God

TODAY'S PASSAGE

BIBLE VERSION

TODAY'S TOPIC

NOTES

KEY VERSES

PRAYER

KEY POINTS

APPLICATION

Let's get things done!

TOP PRIORITIES	IDEAS	WATER

TO-DO	THOUGHTS	FOOD

BREAKFAST	LUNCH	DINNER

	RELAXING THINGS TO DO	GOALS

FITNESS	NOTES	

SKETCH

Notes

Notes

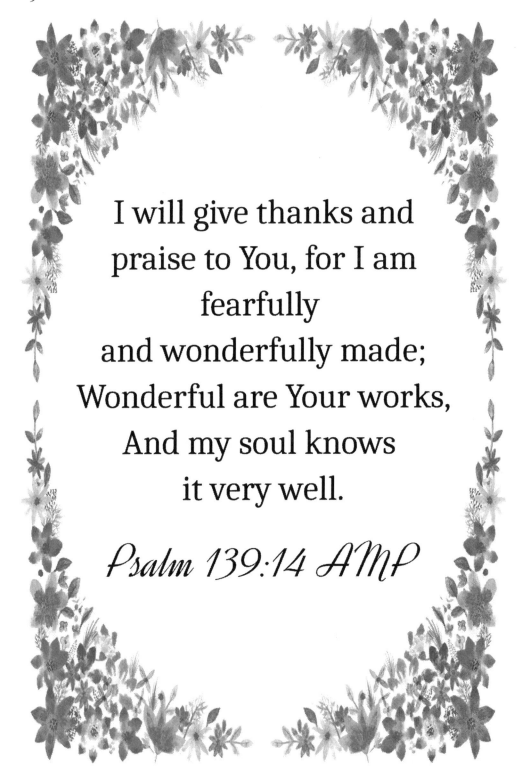

I will give thanks and
praise to You, for I am
fearfully
and wonderfully made;
Wonderful are Your works,
And my soul knows
it very well.

Psalm 139:14 AMP

Day 9:

Fearfully

and

wonderfully

made

Fearfully and wonderfully made

Focus of the day

God made no mistakes when he created you. He is God who never fails or makes mistakes. Everything about you was thought about and executed perfectly before you were created. God is deeply in love with you and admires everything about you, down to the smallest detail. You are mysteriously complex and marvelous. To God, you are everything, and today I pray you will begin to view yourself the same way.

Tasks for the day

Spend time with God for 30 minutes.
Write out your strengths and flaws today and give them over to God. Let God help you understand that everything about you is perfect, for God never makes mistakes.
Read Psalm 18; 139; 1 Corinthians 6:19-20.

Let's get moving

Exercise for 30 minutes.
Spend 30 minutes outside.
Drink 1 gallon of water.

Date: _____

Reflection

Today, I am truly grateful for...

_____

_____

_____

What I love about myself...

_____

_____

_____

_____

_____

What I learned about myself today...

_____

_____

_____

_____

_____

I am...

_____

_____

_____

I forgave myself today for...

_____

_____

_____

What I would like to change about myself...

_____

_____

An amazing thing that happened today...

_____

My time with God

DATE

TODAY'S PASSAGE BIBLE VERSION TODAY'S TOPIC

NOTES

KEY VERSES

PRAYER

KEY POINTS

APPLICATION

Let's get things done!

TOP PRIORITIES	IDEAS	WATER

TO-DO	THOUGHTS	FOOD

BREAKFAST | LUNCH | DINNER

	RELAXING THINGS TO DO	GOALS

FITNESS	NOTES	

SKETCH

Notes

Notes

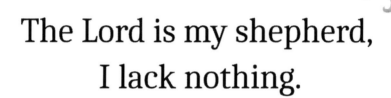

The Lord is my shepherd,
I lack nothing.

Psalm 23:1 NIV

Day 10:

Lacking

nothing

Lacking nothing

Focus of the day

God is your shepherd; in him, you lack nothing.
In God, you have abundance. Therefore, nothing
is missing in you that God cannot give you.
There's no empty space in your heart that God
cannot fill. All your needs, wants, and desires are
met in Him. So, whatever you are seeking,
know that you will find it in God. He will give you
all that you need. We don't have to try to
obtain love, wholeness, or money alone.
Our heavenly Father is on our side, ready
to assist us in whatever we need.

Tasks for the day

Spend time with God for 30 minutes.
What are you lacking today? Present it to God and
know that in Him, you have abundance.
Place your name in each of today's scriptures.
Read Psalms 21; 23; James 1:17.

Let's get moving

Exercise for 30 minutes.
Spend 30 minutes outside.
Drink 1 gallon of water.

Date: ....

Reflection

Today, I am truly grateful for...

_____
_____
_____

What I love about myself...

_____
_____
_____
_____
_____

What I learned about myself today...

_____
_____
_____
_____
_____

I am...

_____
_____
_____

I forgave myself today for...

_____
_____
_____

What I would like to change about myself...

_____
_____
_____

An amazing thing that happened today...

_____

My time with God

DATE

TODAY'S PASSAGE **BIBLE VERSION** **TODAY'S TOPIC**

NOTES

KEY VERSES

PRAYER

KEY POINTS

APPLICATION

Let's get things done!

TOP PRIORITIES	IDEAS	WATER

TO-DO	THOUGHTS	FOOD

BREAKFAST	LUNCH	DINNER

RELAXING THINGS TO DO	GOALS

FITNESS	NOTES

SKETCH

Notes

Notes

Come to me, all
you who are
weary and burdened,
and I will give you rest.
Take my yoke upon you and
learn from me,
for I am gentle
and humble in heart, and
you will find rest
for your souls.

Matthew 11:28-29

NLT

Day 11:

Do nothing day

Do nothing day

Focus of the day

A day of doing nothing can bring much-needed clarity, peace, and awareness of our surroundings and life. So, let's relax and cherish this day the Lord has given us. Dedicate this day to relaxing, and if that's not feasible for you, then aim for a couple of hours instead.

Tasks for the day

Spend time with God for 30 minutes. Take a relaxing bath. Get a manicure and pedicure at a nail salon. Go for a hike or fishing with a close friend. Do whatever relaxing activity you always wanted to do, but never had the time to accomplish. Read Psalm 145.

Let's get moving

Full body stretch for 30 minutes.
Spend 30 minutes outside.
Drink 1 gallon of water and eat only fruits for breakfast.

Date: ....

Reflection

Today, I am truly grateful for...

_____

_____

What I love about myself...

_____

_____

_____

_____

What I learned about myself today...

_____

_____

_____

I am...

_____

_____

I forgave myself today for...

_____

_____

What I would like to change about myself...

_____

_____

An amazing thing that happened today...

_____

My time with God

DATE

TODAY'S PASSAGE   BIBLE VERSION   TODAY'S TOPIC

NOTES

KEY VERSES

PRAYER

KEY POINTS

APPLICATION

Let's get things done!

TOP PRIORITIES	IDEAS	WATER

D:250ML

TO-DO	THOUGHTS	FOOD

| | | BREAKFAST | LUNCH | DINNER |

	RELAXING THINGS TO DO	GOALS

FITNESS	NOTES	

| | | SKETCH |

Notes

Notes

So you also are
complete
through your
union with Christ,
who is the
head over every
ruler and authority.

Colossians 2:10 NLT

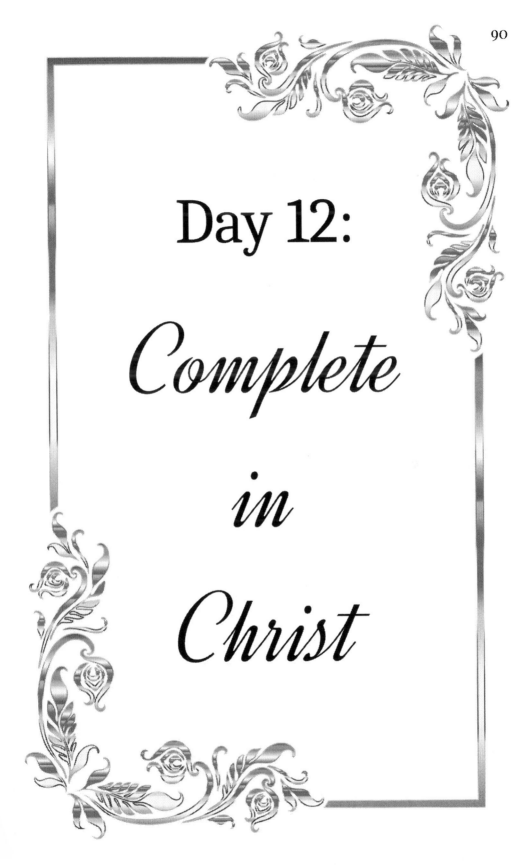

Day 12:

Complete

in

Christ

Complete in Christ

Focus of the day

Have you ever heard someone say,
"You complete me"? People often say it to their
husbands or wives. Though it sounds beautiful,
it can be dangerous to declare this about another
human being. Only God can complete us. God is
whole and lacking nothing. He is the only One
that can fill in every piece of us, even the places
we never realize need filling. In God, you have
everything you need to be complete.

Tasks for the day

Spend time with God for 30 minutes.
What area of your life do you look to another
person or activity to fill? Present those
things to God and allow Him to fill those
areas with Himself. You will obtain peace, joy, and
wholeness as a result.
Read Psalm 21; John 15; Colossians 2.

Let's get moving

Exercise for 30 minutes.
Spend 30 minutes outside.
Drink 1 gallon of water.

Date: _____

Reflection

Today, I am truly grateful for...

_____

_____

_____

What I love about myself...

_____

_____

_____

_____

_____

What I learned about myself today...

_____

_____

_____

_____

I am...

_____

_____

I forgave myself today for...

_____

_____

What I would like to change about myself...

_____

_____

An amazing thing that happened today...

_____

My time with God

DATE

TODAY'S PASSAGE

BIBLE VERSION

TODAY'S TOPIC

NOTES

KEY VERSES

PRAYER

KEY POINTS

APPLICATION

Let's get things done!

TOP PRIORITIES	IDEAS	WATER

TO-DO	THOUGHTS	FOOD

BREAKFAST LUNCH DINNER

	RELAXING THINGS TO DO	GOALS

FITNESS	NOTES	

SKETCH

Notes

Notes

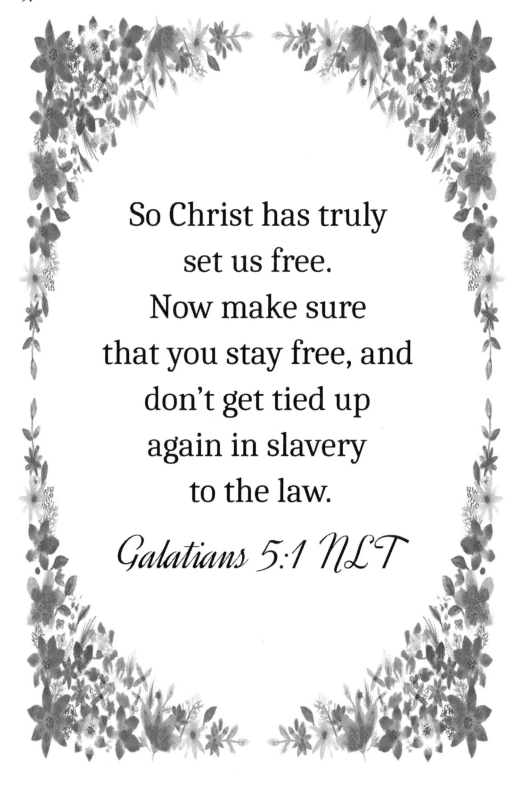

So Christ has truly
set us free.
Now make sure
that you stay free, and
don't get tied up
again in slavery
to the law.

Galatians 5:1 NLT

Day 13:

Set free, walking in freedom

Set free, walking in freedom

Focus of the day

You were set free when Jesus died on the cross.
Your freedom is guaranteed because of Jesus.
However, there are practical things we need
to do to walk in freedom. Reading the word
every day, communicating with God daily, and
surrounding ourselves with godly people and
activities are some of the things that will
help us stay free. So, today, let's practice
walking in freedom.

Tasks for the day

Spend time with God for 30 minutes.
Does your life reflect a life of freedom? What area
of your life is still held in bondage? Talk to God
about whatever is holding you back and hand
those things over to Him, He wants it.
Read Galatians 5.

Let's get moving

Exercise for 30 minutes.
Spend 30 minutes outside.
Drink 1 gallon of water.

Date: _____

Reflection

Today, I am truly grateful for...

_____

_____

_____

What I love about myself...

_____

_____

_____

_____

_____

What I learned about myself today...

_____

_____

_____

_____

_____

I am...

_____

_____

_____

I forgave myself today for...

_____

_____

_____

What I would like to change about myself...

_____

_____

_____

An amazing thing that happened today...

_____

My time with God

DATE

TODAY'S PASSAGE

BIBLE VERSION

TODAY'S TOPIC

NOTES

KEY VERSES

PRAYER

KEY POINTS

APPLICATION

Let's get things done!

TOP PRIORITIES	IDEAS	WATER

TO-DO	THOUGHTS	FOOD

BREAKFAST	LUNCH	DINNER

	RELAXING THINGS TO DO	GOALS

FITNESS	NOTES	

SKETCH

Notes

Notes

You have six days
each week for your
ordinary work,
but the seventh day is
a Sabbath day of
complete rest,
an official day for
holy assembly. It is
the Lord's Sabbath day,
and it must be
observed
wherever you live.

Leviticus 23:3 NLT

Day 14:

Rest/ Sabbath day

Rest/Sabbath day

Focus of the day

Rest. Refocus. Remember.
Rest in God's word today and in His presence.
Worship Him and praise His name today by
thanking Him for being God.
Refocus on God and finish what he told you to
do recently. Take time today to remember how
God came through for you in the past.
Understand that the Sabbath is a gift
from God to us.

Tasks for the day

Spend time with God for 30 minutes.
Praise and worship God today. He is a great God
who has done so much for you. Thank Jesus for
dying on the cross for you. Thank Him for
assisting you on this journey of loving your life.
Honor God by giving Him your day and praise
Him. Read Exodus 16:22-36 NLT and Leviticus 23.

Let's get moving

Dance to worship music for 30 minutes.
Walk for 30 minutes outside.
Drink 1 gallon of water.

Date: _____   *Reflection*

Today, I am truly grateful for...

_____

_____

What I love about myself...

_____

_____

_____

_____

What I learned about myself today...

_____

_____

_____

_____

I am...

_____

_____

I forgave myself today for...

_____

_____

What I would like to change about myself...

_____

_____

An amazing thing that happened today...

_____

My time with God

DATE

TODAY'S PASSAGE

BIBLE VERSION

TODAY'S TOPIC

NOTES

KEY VERSES

PRAYER

KEY POINTS

APPLICATION

Let's get things done!

TOP PRIORITIES	IDEAS	WATER

TO-DO	THOUGHTS	FOOD

BREAKFAST	LUNCH	DINNER

	RELAXING THINGS TO DO	GOALS

FITNESS	NOTES	

SKETCH

Notes

Notes

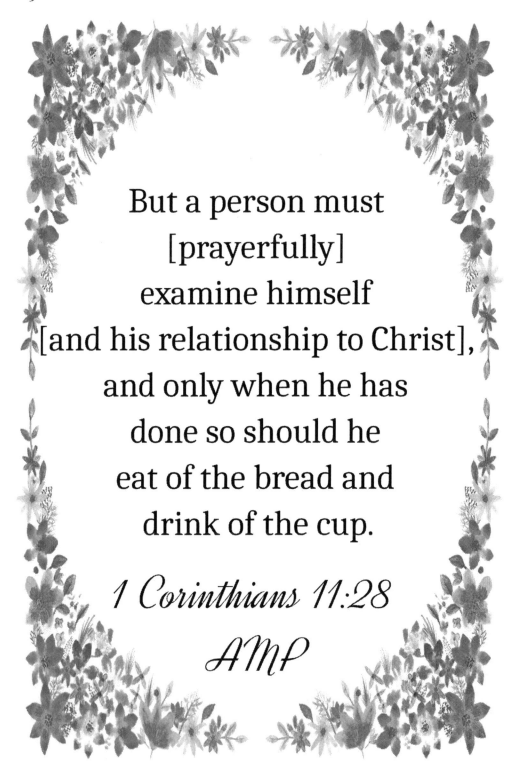

But a person must
[prayerfully]
examine himself
[and his relationship to Christ],
and only when he has
done so should he
eat of the bread and
drink of the cup.

1 Corinthians 11:28

AMP

Day 15:

Examine

your

life

Examine your life

Focus of the day

Today, let's do a life check by examining your life. Who or what in your life may be keeping you from completely loving yourself? Does everything in your life reflect the love of God? Are you allowing God to handle the details of your life? Is there anyone you need to forgive? Take this time to forgive them now and release them to God. Partner with God today and allow Him to assist you as you examine your life.

Tasks for the day

Spend time with God for 30 minutes.
Write out the areas of your life that are not producing peace. Afterward, offer those areas unto God and allow Him to purify them.
Read 1 Chronicles 28:9, Psalm 37: 24-25,
1 Corinthians 11; Hebrews 4:12.

Let's get moving

Exercise for 30 minutes. Spend 30 minutes outside. Drink 1 gallon of water and eat a salad with each meal.

Date: _____ *Reflection*

Today, I am truly grateful for...

_____

_____

_____

What I love about myself...

_____

_____

_____

_____

What I learned about myself today...

_____

_____

_____

_____

I am...

_____

_____

_____

I forgave myself today for...

_____

_____

What I would like to change about myself...

_____

_____

An amazing thing that happened today...

_____

DATE

My time with God

TODAY'S PASSAGE   BIBLE VERSION   TODAY'S TOPIC

NOTES

KEY VERSES

PRAYER

KEY POINTS

APPLICATION

Let's get things done!

TOP PRIORITIES	IDEAS	WATER

TO-DO	THOUGHTS	FOOD

| | | BREAKFAST | LUNCH | DINNER |

	RELAXING THINGS TO DO	GOALS

FITNESS	NOTES	

| | | SKETCH |

Notes

Notes

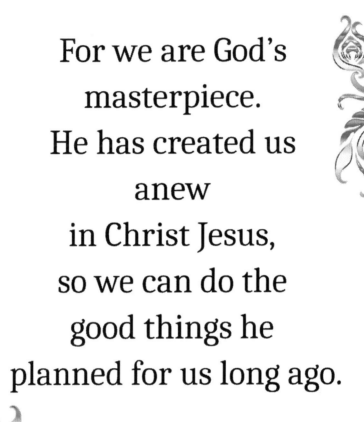

For we are God's
masterpiece.
He has created us
anew
in Christ Jesus,
so we can do the
good things he
planned for us long ago.

Ephesians 2:10
NLT

Day 16:

How do you see yourself?

How do you see yourself?

Focus of the day

Your perspective of yourself determines what you will accept from others, God, and yourself. If you don't have a healthy outlook of yourself, you may allow people to treat you any way they want, talk down to yourself, and have an arduous time accepting God's love for you. Your perspective of yourself should align with God's perspective of you. If the two perspectives do not match, then ask God to give you His perspective and help you heal from the wounds that led to your unhealthy mindset.

Tasks for the day

Spend time with God for 1 hour. Take time today and assess your perspective. Next, partner with God and ask Him to reveal the reasoning behind your perspective. God is the One who can heal and restore you entirely from inception. So, surrender your perspective and accept God's outlook on you. Read Psalm 139 and Isaiah 55:8-9.

Let's get moving

Exercise for 1 hour.
Spend 30 minutes outside.
Drink 1 gallon of water.

Date: _____

Reflection

Today, I am truly grateful for...

_____
_____
_____

What I love about myself...

_____
_____
_____
_____
_____

What I learned about myself today...

_____
_____
_____
_____
_____

I am...

_____
_____
_____

I forgave myself today for...

_____
_____

What I would like to change about myself...

_____
_____

An amazing thing that happened today...

_____

My time with God

DATE

TODAY'S PASSAGE   BIBLE VERSION   TODAY'S TOPIC

NOTES

KEY VERSES

PRAYER

KEY POINTS

APPLICATION

Let's get things done!

TOP PRIORITIES	IDEAS	WATER

TO-DO	THOUGHTS	FOOD

BREAKFAST | LUNCH | DINNER

RELAXING THINGS TO DO | GOALS

FITNESS | NOTES

SKETCH

Notes

Notes

Don't you
realize that
your body is the
temple of the Holy Spirit,
who lives in you and
was given to you by God?
You do not belong to yourself,
for God bought you
with a high price.
So you must honor
God with your body.

1 Corinthians 6:19-20

NLT

Day 17:

God and

your

body/health

God and your body/health

Focus of the day

God cares about every detail of
your life, including your health. God is
ready to provide you with tips and insight on how
to care for your body. He created you, so He knows
what your body needs. Amazingly, we have such a
loving God who has all the answers on our side.
By going to Him, we can eliminate the daunting
task of researching the latest medical discoveries
on achieving optimal health. God has all the
answers for you.

Tasks for the day

Spend time with God for 1 hour. Seek God on what
He says about your health. What skincare and
hair products does He want you to use?
What exercise regimen did He say works best for
you? Beseech Him on whatever you desire to
know about yourself. Read Psalm 37,
Ecclesiastes 11:10; 1 Corinthians 3:16-23; 6.

Let's get moving

Exercise for 1 hour.
Spend 30 minutes outside.
Drink 1 gallon of water.

Date: ....

Reflection

Today, I am truly grateful for...

What I love about myself...

What I learned about myself today...

I am...

I forgave myself today for...

What I would like to change about myself...

An amazing thing that happened today...

My time with God

DATE

TODAY'S PASSAGE   BIBLE VERSION   TODAY'S TOPIC

NOTES

KEY VERSES

PRAYER

KEY POINTS

APPLICATION

Let's get things done!

TOP PRIORITIES	IDEAS	WATER

DC250ML

TO-DO	THOUGHTS	FOOD

| | | BREAKFAST | LUNCH | DINNER |

	RELAXING THINGS TO DO	GOALS

FITNESS	NOTES	

SKETCH

Notes

Notes

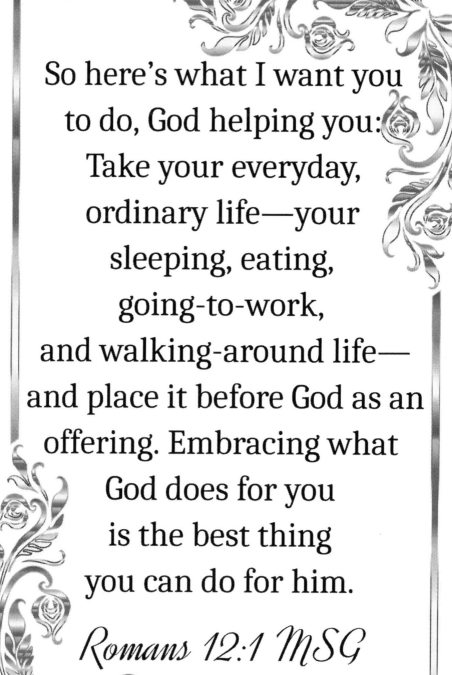

So here's what I want you
to do, God helping you:
Take your everyday,
ordinary life—your
sleeping, eating,
going-to-work,
and walking-around life—
and place it before God as an
offering. Embracing what
God does for you
is the best thing
you can do for him.

Romans 12:1 MSG

Day 18:

Taking care

of

yourself

Taking care of yourself

Focus of the day

Let's assess how you take care of yourself.
Do you buy yourself whatever you need?
Do you create excuses as to why you should
not treat yourself? Do you speak kindly to
yourself? Are you gentle with your body?
Do you consciously consume nutritious foods?
Allow God to assist you in caring for
yourself as He takes care of you.

Tasks for the day

Spend time with God for 1 hour.
Ask God to reveal how He desires you to
treat and care for yourself. Read Psalm 30:2;
Ecclesiastes 3:12-13; Romans 12.

Let's get moving

Exercise for 1 hour.
Spend 30 minutes outside. Drink 1 gallon of
water and eat a fruit bowl for a snack.

Date: _____

Reflection

Today, I am truly grateful for...

What I love about myself...

What I learned about myself today...

I am...

I forgave myself today for...

What I would like to change about myself...

An amazing thing that happened today...

DATE

My time with God

TODAY'S PASSAGE   BIBLE VERSION   TODAY'S TOPIC

NOTES

KEY VERSES

KEY POINTS

PRAYER

APPLICATION

Let's get things done!

TOP PRIORITIES	IDEAS	WATER

TO-DO	THOUGHTS	FOOD

	RELAXING THINGS TO DO	GOALS

FITNESS	NOTES	

		SKETCH

BREAKFAST | LUNCH | DINNER

DC250ML

Notes

Notes

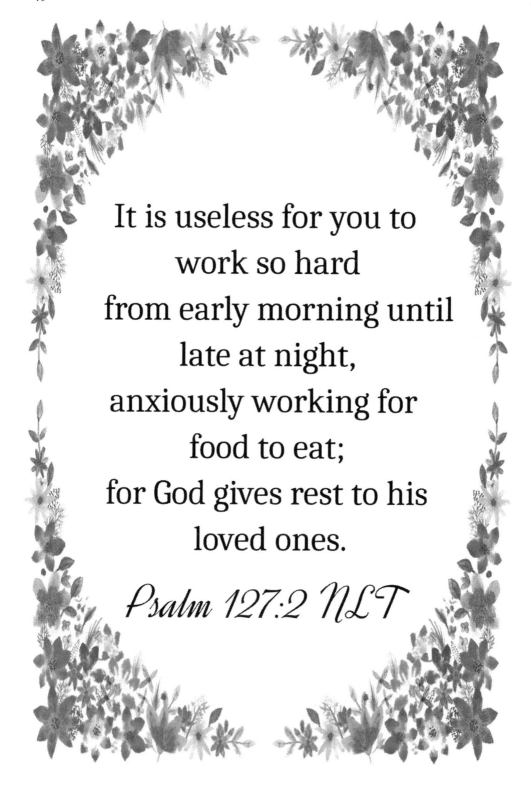

It is useless for you to
work so hard
from early morning until
late at night,
anxiously working for
food to eat;
for God gives rest to his
loved ones.

Psalm 127:2 NLT

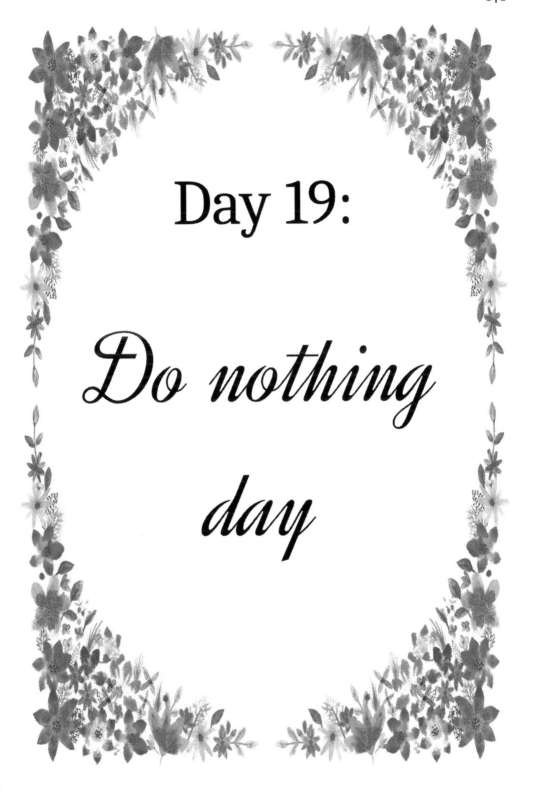

Day 19:

Do nothing day

Do nothing day

Focus of the day

We all need a day to sit back, relax, and enjoy
life. So, today is the day we will pamper
ourselves and give our minds a
break from analyzing different issues.
Also, we will enable our bodies to rest from our
regular day-to-day routines.
Today, be present physically, emotionally,
and spiritually.

Tasks for the day

Spend time with God for 1 hour.
Be obedient to God and complete the relaxing
activity He has been prompting you to do.
He wants you to relax and take care of
yourself today. Read Psalm 100.

Let's get moving

Full body stretch for 1 hour.
Spend 30 minutes outside.
Drink 1 gallon of water and eat your
favorite snack or meal.

Date: _____

Reflection

Today, I am truly grateful for...

_____

_____

What I love about myself...

_____

_____

_____

_____

What I learned about myself today...

_____

_____

_____

_____

I am...

_____

_____

I forgave myself today for...

_____

_____

What I would like to change about myself...

_____

_____

An amazing thing that happened today...

_____

My time with God

DATE

TODAY'S PASSAGE   **BIBLE VERSION**   **TODAY'S TOPIC**

NOTES

KEY VERSES

PRAYER

KEY POINTS

APPLICATION

Let's get things done!

TOP PRIORITIES	IDEAS	WATER

DC250ML

TO-DO	THOUGHTS	FOOD

		BREAKFAST	LUNCH	DINNER

	RELAXING THINGS TO DO	GOALS

FITNESS	NOTES	

		SKETCH

Notes

Notes

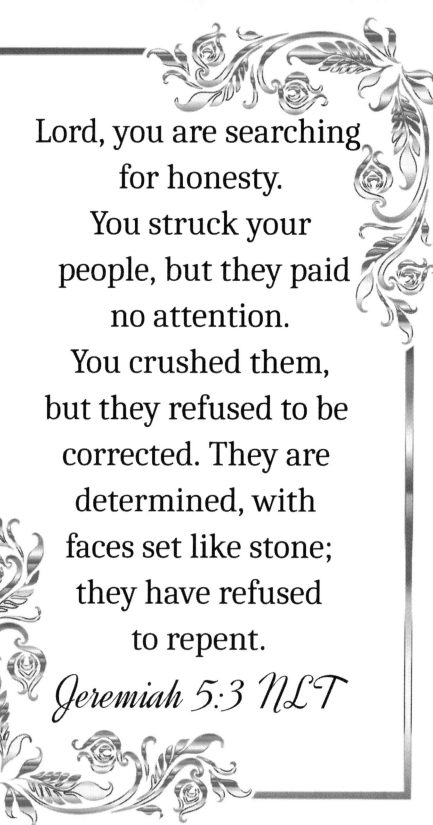

Lord, you are searching
for honesty.
You struck your
people, but they paid
no attention.
You crushed them,
but they refused to be
corrected. They are
determined, with
faces set like stone;
they have refused
to repent.

Jeremiah 5:3 NLT

Day 20:

Be honest

with God

Be honest with God

Focus of the day

God desires your honesty. Whatever you are feeling, let God know. Tell God if you are angry at Him, disappointed, tired, weary, frustrated, sad, or anything else. You will not make Him angry. He is your heavenly father, and He sincerely cares about your feelings.

Tasks for the day

Spend time with God for 1 hour. Tell God how you are feeling today. Let Him comfort you and navigate you through your feelings. As you grasp the importance of honesty with God, you will begin to perceive God accurately due to your encounters with Him. You will recognize that you are altogether cherished and loved by God even when you are disheartened. Give it all to God. Also, find scriptures for what you are feeling. Read Psalm 7:9; 23; 27; 56; 42; Jeremiah 5:3.

Let's get moving

Exercise for 1 hour.
Spend 30 minutes outside.
Drink 1 gallon of water.

Date: ....

Reflection

Today, I am truly grateful for...

_____

_____

_____

What I love about myself...

_____

_____

_____

_____

_____

What I learned about myself today...

_____

_____

_____

_____

_____

I am...

_____

_____

_____

I forgave myself today for...

_____

_____

_____

What I would like to change about myself...

_____

_____

An amazing thing that happened today...

_____

DATE

My time with God

TODAY'S PASSAGE   BIBLE VERSION   TODAY'S TOPIC

NOTES

KEY VERSES

PRAYER

KEY POINTS

APPLICATION

Let's get things done!

TOP PRIORITIES	IDEAS	WATER

DC250ML

TO-DO	THOUGHTS	FOOD

		BREAKFAST	LUNCH	DINNER

	RELAXING THINGS TO DO	GOALS

FITNESS	NOTES	

		SKETCH

Notes

Notes

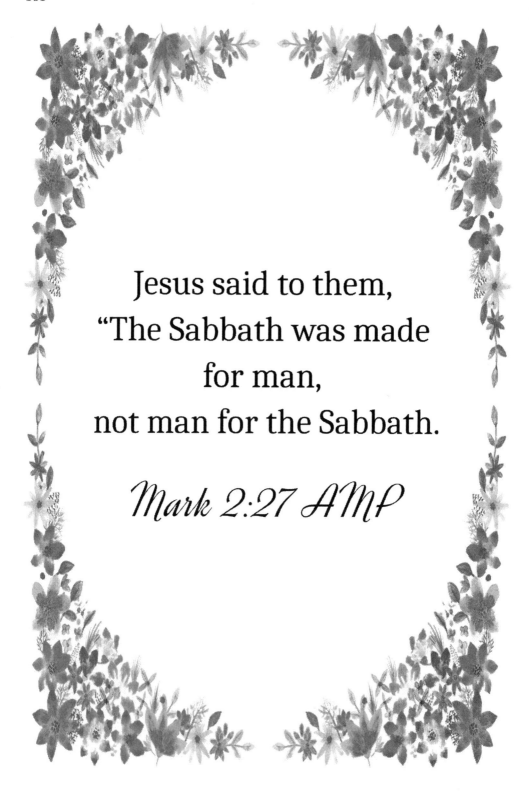

Jesus said to them,
"The Sabbath was made
for man,
not man for the Sabbath.

Mark 2:27 AMP

Day 21:

Rest/ Sabbath

day

Rest/Sabbath day

Focus of the day

This Sabbath day is a day the Lord has made for us. Let us rejoice today by honoring God and spending time with Him. Wear comfortable loungewear, grab your favorite snack, and relax with God. God values rest and knows how much we will benefit from resting in Him.

Tasks for the day

Spend time with God for 1 hour.
Rest in God and read scriptures on God being your resting place. Play worship music and dance like you are free from all bondage and hindrance. God has given us freedom, so we should treasure this rest day like He intended.
Read Psalm 55; 118:4; Matthew 6:9-13.

Let's get moving

Dance to worship music for 30 minutes.
Walk for 30 minutes outside.
Drink 1 gallon of water.

Date: _____

Reflection

Today, I am truly grateful for...

_____
_____

What I love about myself...

_____
_____
_____
_____

What I learned about myself today...

_____
_____
_____
_____

I am...

_____
_____

I forgave myself today for...

_____
_____

What I would like to change about myself...

_____
_____

An amazing thing that happened today...

_____

DATE

My time with God

TODAY'S PASSAGE   BIBLE VERSION   TODAY'S TOPIC

NOTES

KEY VERSES

PRAYER

KEY POINTS

APPLICATION

Let's get things done!

TOP PRIORITIES	IDEAS	WATER

DC250ML

TO-DO	THOUGHTS	FOOD

| | | BREAKFAST | LUNCH | DINNER |

	RELAXING THINGS TO DO	GOALS

FITNESS	NOTES	

SKETCH

Notes

Notes

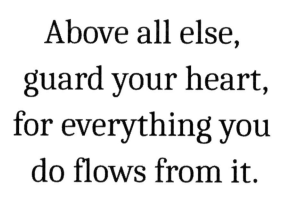

Above all else,
guard your heart,
for everything you
do flows from it.

Proverbs 4:23 NIV

Day 22:

Creating

boundaries

Creating boundaries

Focus of the day

So far, we have been renewed, discovered who God says we are, and learned to trust God with every detail of our lives. Now we must learn to guard it by creating boundaries. Everything we do and who we are comes from the heart. Since our hearts belong to God, we must investigate our lives to see where we can create boundaries to protect our hearts and align with the work God is doing in us through this journey. Creating boundaries looks like being mindful of what we watch and listen to, who we associate with, and how we spend our time. If we are committed to loving ourselves like God, we must adjust how we live.

Tasks for the day

Spend time with God for 1 hour. Ask God what boundaries you should create in your life. What areas of your life need more protection from the world? Read Proverbs 4 and Matthew 15:18-19.

Let's get moving

Exercise for 1 hour. Spend 30 minutes outside. Drink 1 gallon of water and drink a green smoothie.

Date: _____

Reflection

Today, I am truly grateful for...

_____
_____
_____

What I love about myself...

_____
_____
_____
_____
_____

What I learned about myself today...

_____
_____
_____
_____

I am...

_____
_____
_____

I forgave myself today for...

_____
_____

What I would like to change about myself...

_____
_____

An amazing thing that happened today...

_____

My time with God

DATE

TODAY'S PASSAGE

BIBLE VERSION

TODAY'S TOPIC

NOTES

KEY VERSES

PRAYER

KEY POINTS

APPLICATION

Let's get things done!

TOP PRIORITIES	IDEAS	WATER

TO-DO	THOUGHTS	FOOD

BREAKFAST	LUNCH	DINNER

	RELAXING THINGS TO DO	GOALS

FITNESS	NOTES	

SKETCH

1X250ML

Notes

Notes

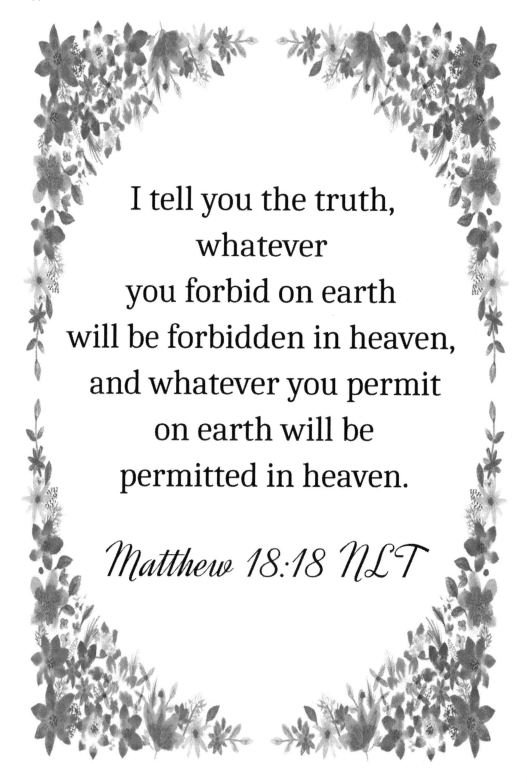

I tell you the truth,
whatever
you forbid on earth
will be forbidden in heaven,
and whatever you permit
on earth will be
permitted in heaven.

Matthew 18:18 NLT

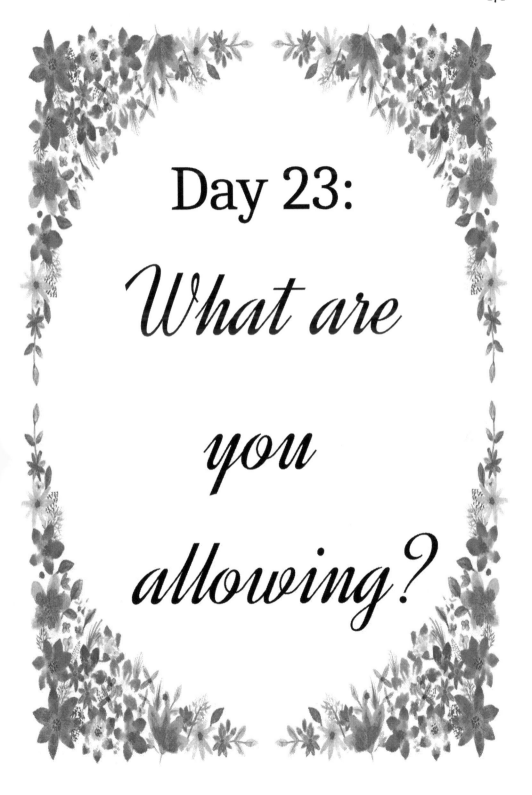

Day 23:

What are

you

allowing?

What are you allowing?

Focus of the day

What are you allowing in your life that does not align with God? Negativity? Emotional bondage? Hopelessness? Doubt? What are you listening to, watching, and reading that goes against who you are? Since we have allowed God to make us completely over on this journey, we must be intentional about what we permit in our lives. We should not be indifferent to what we tolerate in our lives; everything we do should align with God and who we are as children of God.

Tasks for the day

Spend time with God for 1 hour. Everything we take in impacts us and our perspective, whether we realize it or not. So, analyze how you spend your day and remove anything that does not align with the work God is doing in you. Read Matthew 18; 2 Timothy 2; 3:16; Jude 1:17-25.

Let's get moving

Exercise for 1 hour. Spend 30 minutes outside. Drink 1 gallon of water.

Date: _____

Reflection

Today, I am truly grateful for...

_____
_____
_____

What I love about myself...

_____
_____
_____
_____
_____

What I learned about myself today...

_____
_____
_____
_____
_____

I am...

_____
_____
_____

I forgave myself today for...

_____
_____
_____

What I would like to change about myself...

_____
_____

An amazing thing that happened today...

_____

My time with God

DATE

TODAY'S PASSAGE

BIBLE VERSION

TODAY'S TOPIC

NOTES

KEY VERSES

PRAYER

KEY POINTS

APPLICATION

Let's get things done!

TOP PRIORITIES	IDEAS	WATER

D/250ML

TO-DO	THOUGHTS	FOOD

		BREAKFAST	LUNCH	DINNER

	RELAXING THINGS TO DO	GOALS

FITNESS	NOTES	

		SKETCH

Notes

Notes

Therefore, dear
brothers and sisters,
you have no obligation
to do what your sinful
nature urges you to do.
For if you live by its dictates,
you will die.
But if through the power
of the Spirit you put to
death the deeds of
your sinful nature,
you will live.

Romans 8:12-13 NLT

Day 24:

What/who

needs to go

What/Who needs to go?

Focus of the day

Has God been nudging you to change jobs, friends, church, or dating habits? If you have not made those changes, let's do it today. God is giving you those instructions for a reason. He has a purpose and plan for your life that is for your benefit and His eminence. Trust God with every facet of your life and allow Him to remove whomever and whatever He needs to. If there's anything in your life that did not come from God and is leading you away from Him, then let it go.

Tasks for the day

Spend time with God for 1 hour.
You don't have to take every promotion, meeting, invitation, or comment that is presented to you. If God's hand is not on it, you should walk away.
Read Romans 8.

Let's get moving

Exercise for 1 hour.
Spend 30 minutes outside. Drink 1 gallon of water and eat a salad with each meal.

Date: _____

Reflection

Today, I am truly grateful for...
_____
_____
_____

What I love about myself...
_____
_____
_____
_____

What I learned about myself today...
_____
_____
_____
_____

I am...
_____
_____

I forgave myself today for...
_____
_____

What I would like to change about myself...
_____
_____

An amazing thing that happened today...
_____

My time with God

DATE

TODAY'S PASSAGE   BIBLE VERSION   TODAY'S TOPIC

NOTES

KEY VERSES

PRAYER

KEY POINTS

APPLICATION

Let's get things done!

TOP PRIORITIES	IDEAS	WATER

DC250ML

TO-DO	THOUGHTS	FOOD

| | | BREAKFAST | LUNCH | DINNER |

	RELAXING THINGS TO DO	GOALS

FITNESS	NOTES	

SKETCH

Notes

Notes

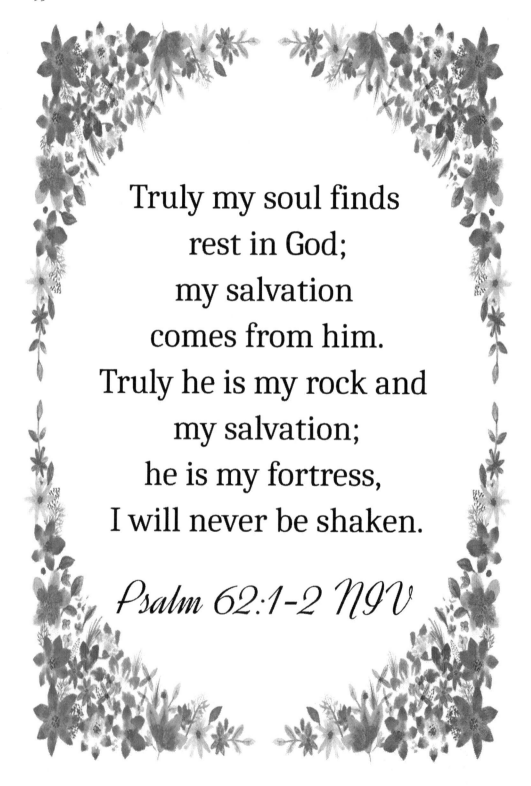

Truly my soul finds
rest in God;
my salvation
comes from him.
Truly he is my rock and
my salvation;
he is my fortress,
I will never be shaken.

Psalm 62:1-2 NIV

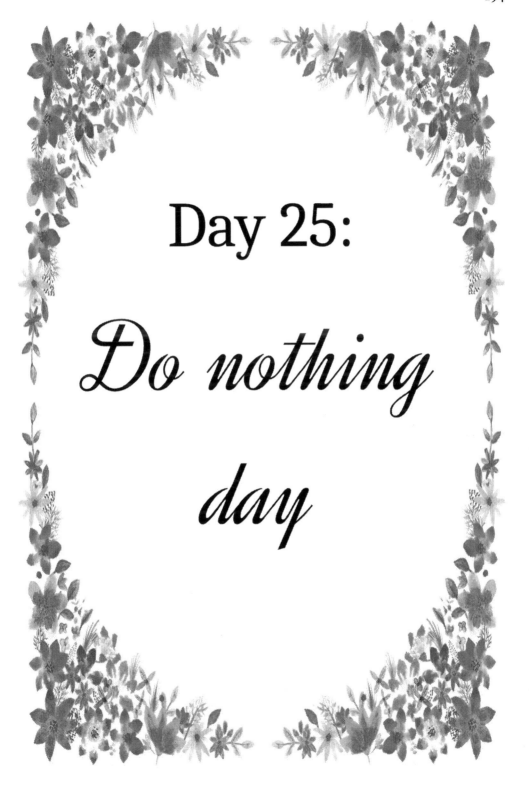

Day 25:

Do nothing

day

Do nothing day

Focus of the day

Doing nothing can bring so much joy to our minds and bodies. It is a time to treat ourselves the way we should be treated. We do not have to wait for someone else to treat us. The longest relationship we will ever have will be with ourselves. Therefore, we should be the first ones to pamper ourselves. Through this journey, you are beginning to meet the person God always intended you to be, who deserves to be treated with tenderness. So, let's treat and pamper ourselves today.

Tasks for the day

Spend time with God for 1 hour.
Read a fictional book today. Buy that item you have wanted for some time now. Take a road trip to a park or a scenic area and encompass the nature around you. Read Psalm 62.

Let's get moving

Full body stretch for 1 hour.
Spend 30 minutes outside.
Drink 1 gallon of water and only eat plant-based meals today.

Date: _____

Reflection

Today, I am truly grateful for...

_____
_____
_____

What I love about myself...

_____
_____
_____
_____
_____

What I learned about myself today...

_____
_____
_____
_____
_____

I am...

_____
_____
_____

I forgave myself today for...

_____
_____
_____

What I would like to change about myself...

_____
_____

An amazing thing that happened today...

_____

DATE _____

My time with God

TODAY'S PASSAGE	BIBLE VERSION	TODAY'S TOPIC

NOTES

_____
_____
_____
_____
_____
_____
_____
_____
_____
_____

KEY VERSES

PRAYER

_____
_____
_____
_____
_____
_____

KEY POINTS

_____
_____
_____
_____
_____
_____
_____

APPLICATION

Let's get things done!

TOP PRIORITIES	IDEAS	WATER

TO-DO	THOUGHTS	FOOD

		BREAKFAST	LUNCH	DINNER

	RELAXING THINGS TO DO	GOALS

FITNESS	NOTES	

		SKETCH

Notes

Notes

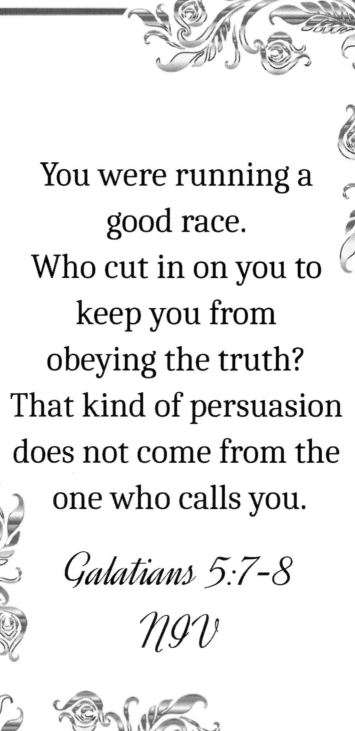

You were running a
good race.
Who cut in on you to
keep you from
obeying the truth?
That kind of persuasion
does not come from the
one who calls you.

Galatians 5:7-8
NIV

Day 26:

Who said it?

Who said it?

Focus of the day

Where did those repeated thoughts in your mind come from? Is it adding fruit to your life or pain? Our minds are filled with words we probably never spoke to ourselves, yet we believe them. We may not know where these thoughts or beliefs came from either. Futhermore, these thoughts may have been written off as part of our identity. Today, we are going investigate those thoughts and beliefs.

Tasks for the day

Spend time with God for 1 hour. What beliefs or thoughts have been weighing you down? Did they come from God, you, people, or the enemy? Surrender your beliefs and thoughts to God today and enable Him to reveal what is from Him and what is not. Read Galatians 5 and 1 Peter 1:13-25.

Let's get moving

Exercise for 1 hour.
Spend 30 minutes outside.
Drink 1 gallon of water.

Date: _____

Reflection

Today, I am truly grateful for...

_____

_____

_____

What I love about myself...

_____

_____

_____

_____

_____

What I learned about myself today...

_____

_____

_____

_____

I am...

_____

_____

_____

I forgave myself today for...

_____

_____

_____

What I would like to change about myself...

_____

_____

An amazing thing that happened today...

_____

_____

_____

My time with God

TODAY'S PASSAGE	BIBLE VERSION	TODAY'S TOPIC

NOTES

_____
_____
_____
_____
_____
_____
_____
_____
_____
_____

PRAYER

_____
_____
_____
_____
_____
_____
_____
_____
_____
_____
_____
_____

KEY VERSES

KEY POINTS

APPLICATION

Let's get things done!

TOP PRIORITIES	IDEAS	WATER

TO-DO	THOUGHTS	FOOD

		BREAKFAST	LUNCH	DINNER

	RELAXING THINGS TO DO	GOALS

FITNESS	NOTES	

		SKETCH

207

Notes

Notes

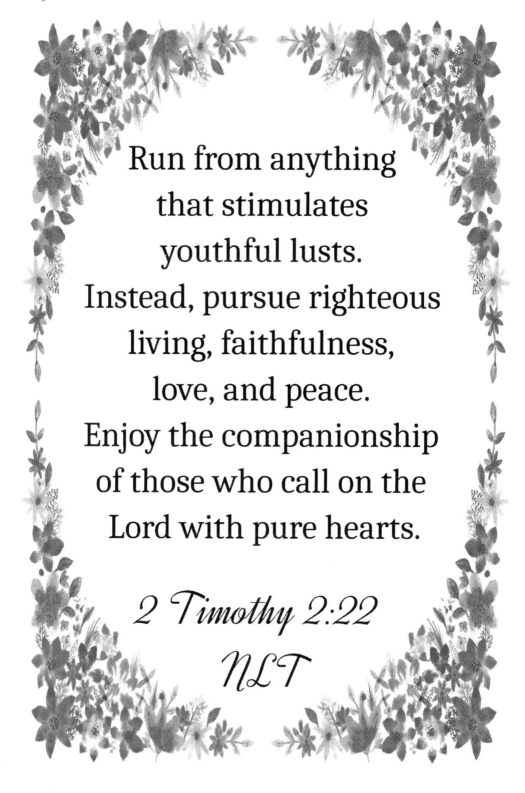

Run from anything
that stimulates
youthful lusts.
Instead, pursue righteous
living, faithfulness,
love, and peace.
Enjoy the companionship
of those who call on the
Lord with pure hearts.

2 Timothy 2:22
NLT

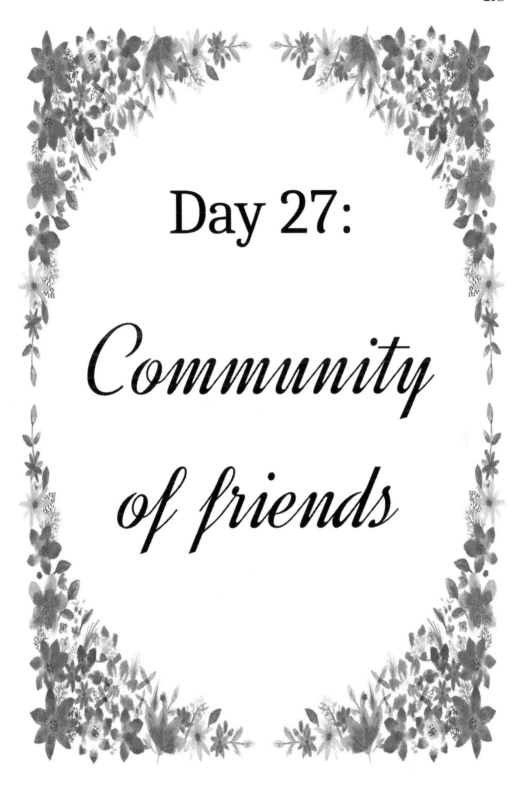

Day 27:

Community

of friends

Community of friends

Focus of the day

The people we associate with can
hinder or encourage our growth. Does your
community of friends encourage you to grow
or stunt your development? Do your friendships
mirror God in any way? Let God to connect you
with a community that honors Him and has
a relationship with Him. Being surrounded by
like-minded individuals will benefit
you in the end.

Tasks for the day

Spend time with God for 1 hour. Evaluate your
community of friends to detect if they are
also aligned with God and your growth. Ask God
to help you view your community through
His eyes. Read Proverbs 12:16; 13:20; 22:24-25;
27:17; 1 Corinthians 15:33; 2 Timothy 2.

Let's get moving

Exercise for 1 hour.
Spend 30 minutes outside.
Drink 1 gallon of water and eat fruit for
breakfast.

Date: ....

Reflection

Today, I am truly grateful for...

_____

_____

What I love about myself...

_____

_____

_____

_____

What I learned about myself today...

_____

_____

_____

_____

I am...

_____

_____

I forgave myself today for...

_____

_____

What I would like to change about myself...

_____

_____

An amazing thing that happened today...

_____

DATE

My time with God

TODAY'S PASSAGE | BIBLE VERSION | TODAY'S TOPIC

NOTES

KEY VERSES

PRAYER

KEY POINTS

APPLICATION

Let's get things done!

TOP PRIORITIES	IDEAS	WATER

TO-DO	THOUGHTS	FOOD

		BREAKFAST	LUNCH	DINNER

	RELAXING THINGS TO DO	GOALS

FITNESS	NOTES	

		SKETCH

DC250ML

Notes

Notes

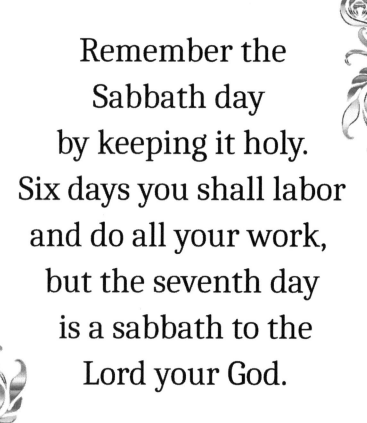

Remember the
Sabbath day
by keeping it holy.
Six days you shall labor
and do all your work,
but the seventh day
is a sabbath to the
Lord your God.

Exodus 20:8-10

NIV

Day 28:

Rest/

Sabbath

day

Rest/Sabbath day

Focus of the day

Rest and focus on God today. This is your day of peace and ease, so receive the peace of God and let Him comfort you with His presence.
Also, look over your previous prayers, dreams, and testimonies to remember what God has done and what He is about to do.

Tasks for the day

Spend time with God for 1 hour.
Thank God for everything you have, the people around you, and the prayers He has yet to answer.
Thank God for never leaving you. Futhermore, watch videos of other people's testimonies of how God moved in their lives. Read Exodus 20:8-10.

Let's get moving

Dance to worship music for 30 minutes.
Walk for 30 minutes outside.
Drink 1 gallon of water.

Date: _____

Reflection

Today, I am truly grateful for...

_____
_____

What I love about myself...

_____
_____
_____
_____

What I learned about myself today...

_____
_____
_____
_____

I am...

_____
_____
_____

I forgave myself today for...

_____
_____

What I would like to change about myself...

_____
_____

An amazing thing that happened today...

_____

My time with God

DATE ....

TODAY'S PASSAGE	BIBLE VERSION	TODAY'S TOPIC

NOTES

_____

KEY VERSES

PRAYER

KEY POINTS

APPLICATION

Let's get things done!

TOP PRIORITIES	IDEAS	WATER

TO-DO	THOUGHTS	FOOD
		BREAKFAST / LUNCH / DINNER

	RELAXING THINGS TO DO	GOALS

FITNESS	NOTES	
		SKETCH

Notes

Notes

Trust in the Lord
with all your heart;
do not depend
on your own understanding.
Seek his will in all you do,
and he will show you
which path to take.

Proverbs 3:5-6 NLT

Day 29:

Trusting

and

obeying

God

Trusting and obeying God

Focus of the day

There is endless proof throughout scripture, history, and our lives that God can be trusted. Trusting and obeying God is paramount to having a relationship with Him. Your willingness to trust and obey God confirms that you love Him wholeheartedly. Additionally, life with God involves plentiful acts of faith that require total trust and a desire to always obey Him, even when life does not match your expectations. Trust God with everything you have and obey Him the first time He speaks. God will never fail you.

Tasks for the day

Spend time with God for 1 hour.
Do you trust God with all your heart? Is obeying God a priority for you? Ask God to help you trust Him more. Read 1 Samuel 15:22-23; Proverbs 3; Isaiah 40; Romans 10:11.

Let's get moving

Exercise for 1 hour. Spend 30 minutes outside. Drink 1 gallon of water.

Date: _____

Reflection

Today, I am truly grateful for...

_____

_____

_____

What I love about myself...

_____

_____

_____

_____

_____

What I learned about myself today...

_____

_____

_____

_____

_____

I am...

_____

_____

_____

I forgave myself today for...

_____

_____

_____

What I would like to change about myself...

_____

_____

_____

An amazing thing that happened today...

_____

My time with God

DATE

| TODAY'S PASSAGE | BIBLE VERSION | TODAY'S TOPIC |

NOTES

KEY VERSES

PRAYER

KEY POINTS

APPLICATION

Let's get things done!

TOP PRIORITIES	IDEAS	WATER

DC250ML

TO-DO	THOUGHTS	FOOD

| | | BREAKFAST | LUNCH | DINNER |

	RELAXING THINGS TO DO	GOALS

FITNESS	NOTES	

| | | SKETCH |

Notes

Notes

And it is a good thing to
receive wealth from
God and the good
health to enjoy it.
To enjoy your work and
accept your lot in life—this
is indeed a gift from God.
God keeps such people
so busy enjoying life that
they take no time to
brood over the past.

Ecclesiastes 5:19-20

NLT

Day 30:

Enjoying

life

Enjoying life

Focus of the day

Loving like God produces an enjoyable life. Peace, purpose, confidence, joy, and love will inhabit you as you live as God intended. You will have more confidence in your decision-making ability and experience quality conversations with people. You will notice increased patience and an internal peace that brings daily joy. Also, you will have unshakable assurance in your identity and purpose. Those are distinguishable life changes when you surrender to God and His perfect will. So, continue to love like God and experience an extraordinary life.

Tasks for the day

Spend time with God for 1 hour. Follow God with your whole heart and live as He intended. Embrace the love of God and love your life. Read Psalm 37:23-24; Ecclesiastes 5:19-20; Jeremiah 29:13; Mark 12:30.

Let's get moving

Exercise for 1 hour. Spend 30 minutes outside. Drink 1 gallon of water and eat a salad with each meal.

Date: _____

Reflection

Today, I am truly grateful for...

_____
_____

What I love about myself...

_____
_____
_____
_____

What I learned about myself today...

_____
_____
_____
_____

I am...

_____
_____

I forgave myself today for...

_____
_____

What I would like to change about myself...

_____
_____

An amazing thing that happened today...

_____

DATE

My time with God

TODAY'S PASSAGE   BIBLE VERSION   TODAY'S TOPIC

NOTES

KEY VERSES

PRAYER

KEY POINTS

APPLICATION

Let's get things done!

TOP PRIORITIES	IDEAS	WATER

TO-DO	THOUGHTS	FOOD
		BREAKFAST · LUNCH · DINNER

	RELAXING THINGS TO DO	GOALS

FITNESS	NOTES	
		SKETCH

Notes

Notes

Notes

Notes

Notes

Notes

Notes

Notes

Scriptures when you feel...

Unloved

John 3:16
1 John 3:1
Mark 12:28-34
Psalm 18
1 Corinthians
13:4-7
1 John 4:8-10
Romans 8:38-39
Ephesians 3:17-19

Anxious/Depressed

Philippians 4:6-7
Matthew 6
1 Peter 5:7
Psalm 3
Deuteronomy 31:8
Jeremiah 29:11
Psalm 34:18
2 Corinthians 1:3-7

Afraid/Fearful

Isaiah 41:10-14
2 Timothy 1:7
Joshua 1:9
Psalm 23
Psalm 91
Psalm 27
Psalm 34:4-8
Psalm 56

Weary/Tired

Matthew 11:28-30
Isaiah 40:28-31
Galatians 6:9
Psalm 46:1
Isaiah 41:10
2 Chronicles 16:9
Psalm 55:22

***Tip:** Put on the armor of God, Ephesians 6:10-17, and pray the Lord's prayer, Matthew 6:9-13, everyday.

Scriptures when you feel...

Inadequate

1 Corinthians 2:1-5
Ephesians 1:3-14
Psalm 139
Psalm 21
2 Corinthians
12:9-10
Ephesians 2:10

Under attack

Psalm 91
Nehemiah 2:20
Matthew 15:13
Isaiah 54:17
Exodus 14:13-14
Psalm 118:17
Ephesians 6:10-20
Mark 11:22-25
2 Corinthians 10:3-5

Disappointed

Romans 8
Psalm 10
Isaiah 55:8-9
Habakkuk 2:2-3
Proverbs 16:9
Psalm 34:18

Confused

1 Corinthians 14:33
1 John 4:4-6
Galatians 5

Lonely

Deuteronomy
31:6
Philippians 4:13
1 Samuel 12:22
Psalm 25
Matthew 28:20

Made in the USA
Columbia, SC
01 October 2023

23625494R00139